WITHDRAWN

BEAUTY AND
THE BUSINESS

Tana Reiff

American Guidance Service, Inc.
Circle Pines, Minnesota 55014-1796
1-800-328-2560

Working for Myself

Clean as a Whistle
Cooking for a Crowd
Crafting a Business
The Flower Man
The Green Team
Handy All Around
Other People's Pets
You Call, We Haul
Your Kids and Mine

Cover Illustration: James Balkovek
Cover Design: Ina McInnis
Text Designer: Diann Abbott

Library of Congress Catalog Number: 94-076141
ISBN 0-7854-1106-2 (Previously ISBN 1-56103-903-9)
Product Number 40831
Printed in the United States of America
A 0 9 8 7 6 5 4 3 2

CONTENTS

Chapter

CHAPTER 1

Beautiful for the Prom

"One more dab of gel and you're done!" Jackie said.

She was doing Taria's hair. The girl lived up the street. She was getting ready to go to the prom that night. Her mom watched every move as Jackie combed out the girl's hair.

"She looks beautiful," said Taria's mom. "More beautiful than *I* ever looked for a prom!"

Jackie smiled. Taria *did* look beautiful. She was pretty to begin with. Now, with hundreds of curls around her face and down her back, she glowed like the sun.

"Who are you going to the prom with?" Jackie asked.

"Robert Tenby," said the girl.

"Well, I hope you have a wonderful time," Jackie smiled. "I hope you never forget this night."

Just then, Jackie's nine-year-old daughter Salina came in. "I'm going over to the store," said the little girl.

"OK," Jackie told her. "You look both ways before you cross the street, hear me? And come right back home."

"OK, Mom," said her daughter as she skipped off.

"Do you remember your high school prom?" Taria's mom asked Jackie.

Jackie wished the subject had been dropped. But she answered the question. "No, I didn't go to the prom," she said. "I *wanted* to go. I even had a beautiful purple gown all ready. Then I made my first big mistake. I got mad one day and just dropped out of school. The school wouldn't let me go to the prom after that. I still have my gown, though. Looks like new to this day."

"Here you are doing hair for the prom," said Taria's mom. "And you never went yourself. How's that for a kick."

"The prom was a long time ago," said Jackie with a little smile. "It doesn't matter anymore. What *does* matter is that I didn't finish school."

"At least you had a baby," said Taria.

Jackie had to laugh. "Oh, yeah. That was my *second* big mistake. Not her— Salina's great—but ending up a single mom was bad news. I married the wrong guy for the wrong reasons. It didn't last long. Now you know why Salina never knew her father."

"You seem to do OK for the two of you, though," said Taria's mom. "You get by with your job at Burger Bazaar. You don't have it so bad, it seems to me."

"I don't want to flip burgers my whole life," said Jackie. "I wish I could be a real hairdresser. I'd like to make a living at it. That used to be my dream."

"Why isn't it *still* your dream?" Taria asked her.

"Well, I would have to go to a cosmetology school. I would have to get my license. Without a high school diploma and money, I can't think about all that."

"There are ways," said Taria's mom. "You can still get your diploma. And then maybe you can dig up some money to go to cosmetology school."

"That all seems a little far for me to reach," said Jackie. "Maybe you're right. I really don't have it so bad the way things are. Could be a lot worse!"

"Hey, you could be out in the street," said Taria's mom. "But that doesn't mean you can't make your life better. It's not too late, you know."

Jackie handed Taria a mirror. "How do you like the back, honey?"

"I look like a princess!" Taria said.

"Now, I want you and Robert to stop by here tonight, you hear?" Jackie said. "I want to take a picture of you in your prom gown."

Taria's mom started to hand Jackie some money. The same hairstyle would have cost three times that much in a salon. Still, Jackie wouldn't take the money. "No, this is on me. I do all my neighbors' hair for fun," she said.

That night Salina stayed over at her friend's house. Jackie ate dinner alone. Then Taria and Robert stopped by. Jackie just about cried when she saw them. "Oh, you're *more* than a princess, honey. You two look like a king and queen!"

After they left, Jackie sat down to watch a TV show. But her mind was somewhere else. *If only, if only, if only* kept going through her head. *If only* she hadn't been hanging out with Salina's father ten years ago. *If only* she hadn't had a baby so young. *If only* she had finished school. *If only* she had taken cosmetology classes back then.

Instead, Jackie was out of money until her next paycheck. Maybe her life wasn't so bad. But it wasn't so *good* either. She hoped that she wouldn't have to spend her whole life that way—crying over what might have been.

There was a time when she dreamed about what she would do with her life. She tried to remember when she had stopped dreaming. Then she had a thought. Maybe dreaming was what she was starting to do again right now.

C H A P T E R   2

The First Step

Jackie was styling the hair on a fake head. When she was finished, the teacher came over to take a look. "Good job, Jackie. Just even out that left side." Jackie fixed the left side. The teacher signed Jackie's skill sheet.

Cosmetology school was like another world to Jackie. Ever since high school she had wondered what it would be like. Now she knew.

Not long after Taria's prom, Jackie had come here to ask about the program. They told her she would need a GED, the high school equivalency diploma. Jackie wasn't happy to hear that. "I'll never make it to cosmetology school," she told herself over and over.

But she stopped herself from thinking like that. She decided she at least had to try. For years she had been pretty sure she would have to face the GED sooner or later. If she wanted to become a real hairstylist, she would have to face it now.

So she went to the adult center while Salina was at her grandmother's. *"I'm going to make it,"* she told herself. She had to say that over and over again to make it sink in.

Some of the night classes were really hard. Jackie was tired after working every evening at Burger Bazaar. Sometimes when she looked at her book right side up, the print looked upside down. But the teacher was always ready to help. With a little extra thinking Jackie got through the hard parts.

GED day came. Jackie spent the day taking the five tests. Then she went home and waited.

A few days later, the telephone call came. Jackie held her breath. "You passed!" the teacher told her.

"Are you sure you called the right number?" Jackie laughed.

"Of course I did, Jackie," said the teacher. "Congratulations! You are now a high school graduate."

Jackie went back to the beauty school. "I really want to study here," she told the supervisor, Mrs. Stevens. "But I don't know how to pay for it."

"The government has some special programs," Mrs. Stevens said. "We should have no problem getting you a job training grant. It will pay for everything. Just hang onto your job until you become a licensed cosmetologist."

"You mean that I really *can* go to

cosmetology school?" Jackie cried.

"You need 1,500 hours of class time," said Mrs. Stevens. "You'll be here eight hours a day. Your only days off will be weekends and holidays. Do you think you can do that?"

Jackie knew this would be a big push. But she was up for it. She was on a roll. She had more drive now than ever in her whole life.

"Yes, I think I can do that," she told Mrs. Stevens.

"Then you should be here Monday morning at 9:00."

Jackie thought she might miss a day now and then. She didn't. Beauty school was work, but it was fun. She went every day, five days a week. She had to get her 1,500 hours in. And five nights a week she flipped burgers.

Jackie thought she already knew a lot about doing hair. But the very first day at school she found out there was much more to learn. This was cosmetology—

not just hair, but nails and skin, too.

Right away Jackie had to learn the laws of cosmetology. The state had rules for this business. Everyone had to know them.

Next she learned what makes up the hair, nails, and skin. Everyone had to know what they were working on and how to do things safely.

Then came the fun part—styling. The class started with wet styling. Jackie learned how to feel people's hair. How to shampoo a head. How to pin curl and finger wave. How to braid and cornrow and make locks and crown rolls. How to weave hair. How to make French rolls and even flips. How to comb hair out. How to choose and use the right combs. How to put on oils and sprays and gels and all kinds of hair goop.

Next came classes on everything having to do with heat. How to blow dry. How to use a hood dryer. How to use a curling iron, a flat iron, hot rollers, and a hot comb. And how to do it safely.

After that came classes on how to give a perm. How to make spirals and spiky curls. And how to relax hair that was already curly.

A big part of the program had to do with cutting hair. How to use scissors, a razor, clippers, and thinning shears. How to do short cuts, crops, layers, tapers, and feathered bangs. How to do the popular cuts that everyone would ask for.

Even more time went to hair color. At first Jackie thought, "Forty hours just on color?" But she was glad for all that time. She didn't want to turn anyone's hair purple when all they wanted was a nice soft gray color.

A different teacher taught the last part of the course. In those classes, Jackie learned to give a facial. She learned to arch eyebrows and get rid of hair. She loved the classes on makeup. Last of all she learned to do nails. Manicures for fingers. Pedicures for toes. How to file.

How to color. How to put on fake nails.

Full-time beauty school took Jackie a whole year. But for the past ten years, going to school at all had seemed like a far-off dream. Now Jackie could almost reach out and touch it. She knew that it was just one step after another, one day at a time.

CHAPTER 3

A License and a Job

Near the end of the program, the cosmetology students went out to visit real salons. Jackie visited two. One was very small. Only four people worked there. The people who worked there were friendly. The place was quiet. Jackie liked it right away.

The second salon was downtown. It was called Hair Circus. Jackie counted 20 full chairs, with 20 stylists working.

The manager, Alonzo, said there were that many at night, too. Jackie thought the name Hair Circus fit the place just right. That day the big salon seemed *too* big to Jackie.

But she went back to Hair Circus for a second visit. This time, Jackie styled someone's hair. Alonzo loved her work. "You style hair like an angel from heaven."

"I didn't know angels styled hair!" Jackie laughed.

She and Alonzo could joke around like that. It made Jackie feel like part of the place. She began to like the feel of the big salon. Still, she never came right out and told Alonzo that she wanted to work there.

Back at the school, Jackie checked the job board. She always looked for a card from Hair Circus.

The end of the school year came. Her classes were all over. But Jackie wasn't finished. If she wanted to work in the beauty field, she needed a license. To get it, she had to pass the state board exam.

The test had two parts. One part was to write answers. One part was to show what you could do.

There was a time when Jackie would have feared the written test. But after passing the GED, she wasn't afraid. Besides, she was ready.

She didn't feel so sure about the second part. A man watched her work on a fake head. He took notes as Jackie worked. By the end, the head had a beautiful do. Jackie knew she had done just fine.

It took time for the papers to get through the state. But then, at last, two months after the board exam, Jackie got her cosmetology license.

She hung the license on the kitchen wall. There it was, with her name and picture right on it. She looked at it ten times a day. It would stay there until Jackie found a job. Then she would take it to the salon.

Jackie called her mom. "I shouldn't have a party till I find a job," Jackie said. "But I'm going to anyway!"

Then she asked all her neighbors to come. She had done everyone's hair so many times. She wanted them all there to celebrate with her.

Jackie baked cakes and cookies all day. She made a fruit punch. She and Salina cut pictures of great hairdos out of magazines. They hung them up all over the apartment.

People started showing up for the party. Many of them brought her gifts.

"Will you still do my hair now that you've got your license?" Taria asked Jackie.

"Sure, honey," Jackie said. "But you'll have to bring yourself down to a salon when I get a job!"

Jackie played music real loud. Everyone danced and had a good time. Jackie hadn't had that much fun for a long time. Maybe she hadn't even had that much fun in high school.

The next week Jackie went down to the beauty school. Every day she checked the job board. Every day she looked for a card from Hair Circus. Still nothing.

"Are you sure that Hair Circus always tells you when they have a job open?" she asked Mrs. Stevens.

"Oh, yes, they do," said the school supervisor. "But why don't you go visit them again?"

Jackie took the bus downtown to Hair Circus. The place was as busy as always. "I really want to work here," she told Alonzo, the manager.

"We don't have anything open right now," he said. "Tell you what. Give me your number and I'll let you know if something opens up."

"Really?" Jackie couldn't believe Alonzo would do that.

"I just put on a new girl about two weeks ago," said Alonzo. "She had a following from another salon. That means she brings in new clients to Hair Circus. But I like your work better than hers. I would have picked you if I knew you wanted to work here."

"Why wasn't there a card on the job board?"

"Because that girl walked in the day someone else quit," Alonzo explained. "She was in the right place at the right time, I guess."

"Well, call me, OK?"

Sure enough, only a week later, Alonzo called. He asked Jackie to come work at Hair Circus. The money wasn't great to start, but there would be tips. Jackie gave Burger Bazaar two weeks' notice. Her boss there was sorry that she was leaving. She had always been one of his best workers.

The first week on the new job, Jackie had fun, even though her feet felt heavy from standing so much. But the day she cashed her first paycheck from Hair Circus, those same two feet felt just as light as air.

If she hadn't just had a party, she would have had one now. Instead she just kept saying to herself, "Is this really happening to me?"

CHAPTER 4

Hair Circus

Jackie hadn't met a lot of new people since high school. She spent most of her time with Salina when she was little. Jackie took her daughter to the park just about every day back then. As the little ones played, she talked with the other young mothers.

On weekends she saw her mom and her neighbors and her cousins. She hadn't made any real friends at Burger Bazaar. Most of the workers there were much younger—just kids, really.

Working at Hair Circus was a new thing for Jackie. She liked the idea of everyone working together. But, because it was new to her, she didn't always do and say the right things.

She didn't like Ivan, for example. He was the guy who worked beside her. That was clear the first day she met him. Even so, she should have kept her mouth shut.

"He's such a little jerk." That's what Jackie said about Ivan to the woman she was working on. The woman didn't say anything.

Jackie finished styling the woman's hair. The woman went to pay. Alonzo asked her, "How was everything?"

The woman answered, "My hair is fine. But that Jackie is saying things about your other stylists."

Alonzo was not happy to hear that. "Thank you for telling me," he told the woman. "I'll take care of it. I hope you'll come back again."

"If I do, I'll ask for someone else," the customer said.

After she left, Alonzo came over to Jackie. "We can't be talking about each other," he told her. "Would you want another hairdresser to be saying things about *you*?"

Jackie wished she could sink into the floor. "I was out of line," she said. "It won't happen again."

It didn't. But next Jackie got into trouble with Lila, the woman who worked on the other side of her.

Lila was sick the day Carl Morgan came in to get his hair cut. Lila had cut Carl's hair for three years. He never called ahead. He just dropped in and asked for Lila. But Lila wasn't there that day and he wanted his hair cut anyway.

"Jackie," Alonzo said, "can you fit in another haircut today?"

"Sure," Jackie said.

Carl Morgan sat down in Jackie's chair. She felt his hair. "A little dry," she said to him. "You might want an oil treatment today."

"Fine," Carl said. "Go ahead."

Jackie cut his hair and gave him an oil treatment. Carl went crazy over the great job she did.

"I never looked so good!" he said. "I'm going to ask for you from now on." He left Jackie a big tip.

The next time Carl came in he asked for Jackie. Lila couldn't help but see Carl in Jackie's chair. After he left Lila said, "What do you think you're doing, taking Carl away from me? He's a good tipper!"

"I didn't take him away from you," Jackie said. "He asked for me."

But Lila was still angry. Carl came in often. Lila would give Jackie a dirty look every time.

In fact, Carl came in more often than he needed to. Jackie began to think he was coming in to see *her*—not just to get a haircut.

At last one day Carl said, "Hey, Jackie.

You and me, we know each other pretty well by now. Would you like to go out with me sometime?"

Jackie hadn't been on a real date since Salina was little. She had sort of given up on men. But Carl Morgan seemed nice. Jackie *did* like him. And Hair Circus had no rules about not dating customers. So she said, "OK."

After that Jackie's life *really* changed. She started seeing Carl every week, then every night. When they decided to get married, no one was surprised. Jackie hadn't thought about getting married again since the days with Salina's father. Carl was a nice guy with a good job. The idea of marrying him felt right.

Not only did Jackie and Carl get married, but they also bought a house. It had three bedrooms, a small yard, and even a basement.

Carl had two sons living with him. All of a sudden Salina had two brothers. And Jackie had a new husband, a new home, and three kids. Now she had plenty of people around her every single night of the week.

She also had a job that seemed to give her a new problem every day.

CHAPTER 5

Running Away from the Circus

Alonzo was the manager of Hair Circus but not the owner. One day he called a meeting of all the stylists. The owner of Hair Circus wanted Alonzo to tell everyone about a new plan.

"You'll be getting paid in a new way starting Tuesday," Alonzo explained. "You won't get paid by the hour anymore. From now on you'll get paid by the job. You'll get a share of all the money you bring in for Hair Circus."

Jackie wasn't sure she liked the sound of this. "Say that Lila and I are both here for eight hours. Are you telling us that we might get paid different amounts?"

"That's right," said Alonzo. He didn't seem thrilled. But he had to carry out the plan, like it or not. After all, *he* worked for the owner, too. "Think of it this way," he added. "Suppose you have a really busy day. Then you would make *more* than you did before."

"But what if the weather's bad and no one shows up?" Lila asked. "Then we sit here for nothing. That doesn't seem fair."

"The owner thinks this *is* the fair way," said Alonzo. "If a lot of clients ask for you, you can make out great. Plus, you'll now get a cut on any shampoo that you sell up front."

So that was that. The stylists had to live with the new plan or leave Hair Circus. Ivan left before the new plan even started. Lila didn't leave, but she moaned about it every day. "Would you like cheese and crackers with your whine?" Alonzo asked her.

Jackie didn't know what to expect. She had always been busy. Her old friends came in often, and every week she picked up new clients, like Carl. As it turned out, Jackie made out well on the new plan. At first.

Then one day she was cutting a man's hair. All of a sudden she felt sick. She said, "Excuse me, sir. I'll be right back." She went in the back room and sat down. She took a deep breath. Then she came back to her styling station. Even though she didn't feel good, she finished cutting the man's hair.

That sick feeling came and went over the next few days. Then Jackie knew for sure what was going on.

It had been almost 12 years since she was pregnant with Salina. She had almost forgotten what it felt like. This *did* feel different. A different baby, she thought. A different father, too.

Jackie and Carl were very happy about having a baby. But Jackie was really sick with this one. Many mornings she just couldn't make it to work on time. When she did get there she had to turn clients over to the other stylists sometimes. And she was being paid by the job, not by the hour now. Taking on fewer clients was costing her money.

And the talk! Jackie and Carl didn't want anyone at Hair Circus to know about the baby. Not yet. But the buzz started anyway. Lila must have started it. Every time Jackie walked by, Lila would stop talking. Jackie was sure the talk was about her being pregnant.

One night at home Carl said to Jackie, "I've been thinking. We have that whole basement down there. Maybe we could finish it off. We could make it into a rec room or something."

"I've been doing some thinking about the basement, too," Jackie said. "I've been thinking we could turn it into a little beauty salon. That way, I could work at home, with the baby and all."

Carl really wanted a rec room, but he saw Jackie's point. "Do you think you can make as much money by working at home?"

Jackie thought she could charge less but make more. There was no one to give part of the money to. "I have my own scissors and perm rods and blow dryer," she said. "But I'll have to put out some money to get started. I need a shampoo sink and a styling chair and a styling station and a big mirror. I'll have to buy insurance, too, in case I hurt anyone by mistake or burn the place down."

"It will also cost some money to fix up the basement," said Carl.

"Right. But we both know that it often takes money to make money. So what do you think?" Jackie asked her husband.

"It's OK with me. But we'd better get started before you get too big."

They found a good buy on floor tile. They bought paint on a credit card. Jackie found out about a salon that was going out of business. She bought an old shampoo sink and a styling station and chair from them for next to nothing. The sink needed a new hose, so she bought one at the beauty supply store. While she was there she also bought a new mirror, two shampoo capes, clips, hair pins, and a pair of rubber gloves.

When the basement salon was ready, Jackie broke the news to Alonzo. He was surprised and sorry to see her go. He tried to make a joke of it.

"You *are* good," he told her. "But running your own business is not easy. You'll come crawling back. Just you wait and see."

"I'm much too pregnant to crawl," Jackie laughed.

Yet she knew she would miss some things about Hair Circus. She would miss learning from the other stylists. She would miss getting new clients off the street. She would miss watching how the business ran. Most of all, she would miss her friend Alonzo.

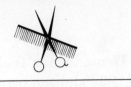

CHAPTER 6

Home But Not Alone

"Hi, Jackie! It's me, Taria!"

"Hi, honey. Come on in and have a seat," said Jackie. "How about this? Here I am doing your hair in my own home again."

"Different home, though," said Taria, looking around.

"*Real* different!" Jackie laughed. "I've got a great husband, four kids, and a business license now." She pointed to her license on the wall. It made her feel proud just to look at it. She showed it to everyone who came in.

"What do you want me to do with your hair today?" Jackie asked.

"I need a straight perm," Taria said. "And I want you to cut my hair so my ears won't stick out."

"I hear you," said Jackie. She always tried to listen to what clients wanted. Then she would add her own ideas for getting the style just right. She started rolling Taria's hair.

"What's your baby's name?" Taria said. She peeked at the sleeping baby.

"Rochelle," said Jackie. "I named her after my Aunt Rochelle."

"Pretty," said Taria.

"So how are you and Robert doing? Are you planning to tie the knot any time soon?" Jackie asked.

"He hasn't asked me yet," said Taria. "Besides, he wants to finish trade school first. He's going to be a carpenter."

"And what about you? What kind of work would *you* like to do?" Jackie asked.

"I used to think about going on to school," said Taria. "But I haven't thought much about that since Robert and I got together."

"Well, don't forget about your own dreams. Sometimes you gotta reach out and grab what you want," said Jackie.

When Taria's perm was finished, Jackie walked over to her desk. "Check or cash today, honey?" she asked.

A look of surprise came over Taria's face. "Oh," she said softly. "I didn't bring checks *or* cash. Now that you're working at home, I thought . . ."

"That's OK," Jackie said. "You don't have to pay me."

"Thanks! You're like the big sister I never had!" said Taria. "See you soon!"

After Taria left, Jackie got to thinking. "It's OK to do a favor for a friend once in a while," she said to herself. "But if I don't charge the people I know, I'll go out of business in no time at all."

The next day Jackie found money from Taria stuck in the door. The note that came with it said, "Sorry I acted like a deadbeat. Hope we're still friends. Love, Taria."

That Sunday a crowd of Jackie's family came over to see the baby. They were about ready to leave when Aunt Rochelle said, "OK, everyone. Let's line up. Before we go Jackie can cut everyone's hair."

Jackie thought Aunt Rochelle was joking—but she wasn't. "You can all hate me," Jackie began. "But I can't cut everyone's hair. For one thing, it would take all night. And for another thing, I've made up my mind. The only people that I do for free are the people who live in this house."

Aunt Rochelle put her hand to her mouth in surprise. She couldn't believe that Jackie would say such a thing. But Jackie was glad that she did.

She didn't see Aunt Rochelle for a long

time after that. But all the others came to her salon, one by one. Every one of them paid for their haircuts and perms and relaxers and braids.

Jackie was doing a cousin's hair one winter day. Baby Rochelle was sleeping in the salon. Right in the middle of a razor cut, the phone rang. The baby started crying.

Jackie answered the phone. "Jackie's salon," she said.

A deep voice—a man's voice—said, "You stop doing business in your home without zoning or I'll torch the place."

Click.

A chill went through Jackie's whole body. The baby cried louder. Jackie couldn't believe what she had heard.

She called the police right away. She had to wait until 6:00 to tell Carl.

"Zoning," said Carl. "We never went to the zoning board about starting up a business in our home."

"There are other people on this block

with home businesses," Jackie said. "I don't think *they* have zoning."

"We better check into it," said Carl.

The next morning Jackie went to City Hall. She found out that, sure enough, she needed a zoning permit. "You should have come here *before* you started your business," she was told.

"How can I get a permit?" Jackie asked the woman at the desk.

Someone from the city would come and take a look at her shop. He or she would want answers to four main questions. *Will the business give the block something it needs? Is there enough parking? Will the business change the way the outside of the house looks? Will the business hurt any other businesses that are not run in homes?*

Weeks later a man from the zoning board came to Jackie's house. He talked with neighbors. He checked for parking places. He looked around the outside of the house. And he checked a list of beauty salons in the area that Jackie's business might be hurting.

"As far as I can see, you should get a permit," said the man. "There's just one thing. You can run your salon only three days a week. There aren't so many problems with in-home businesses if they're not full time."

"Only three days a week?"

"Getting a zoning permit isn't always this easy, you know," said the zoning inspector. "The city doesn't allow home businesses in every part of town. Some streets don't have enough parking. You're lucky."

"Well, it's better than nothing," Jackie said. She did feel more relaxed now. "But what about that man who called on the phone?"

"If he calls again, you do two things," said the zoning inspector. "First you tell him you have a zoning permit. Then you tell him that we can trace his calls. That should get him to stop."

Jackie picked up her zoning permit the next week. The man with the deep voice never called again. Jackie never did find out for sure who he was. But she always wondered about a man who walked by every day. He wore a hood pulled over his head. Everyone else would say hello. This man wouldn't even look Jackie in the eye.

CHAPTER 7

A Business Plan

As Rochelle got a little older, Jackie didn't need to spend as much time with her. That left more time to work. At first most of Jackie's Hair Circus clients had come to her home salon. Some of them still did. Others had stopped.

But Jackie wasn't getting new clients like the walk-ins at Hair Circus. It was hard to fill up even three days a week. She needed to build up her business.

It was also time for Jackie to renew her cosmetology license. To do that she would have to take a class. She really needed one on how to run a salon. So she signed up for the Manager Course. The school had day care for Rochelle.

It was good to be back at the cosmetology school. Most of Jackie's old friends were gone—out working like she was. But most of the teachers she knew were still there.

"Is that you?" said Jackie's favorite teacher when she walked into the school, carrying Rochelle. "You look so different!"

"Oh, it's me," Jackie said. "Been through some changes since I saw you. I worked at Hair Circus. I got married. I got two stepsons in that deal. My husband and I bought a house. Then I had this baby. And now I'm running my own salon in my basement."

"Wow!" said the teacher. "Those *are* a lot of changes. So you're here for the manager's class?"

"Yeah," said Jackie. "I've got my salon set up now, but I need to build up my business. I need more clients to come in. I thought maybe I could learn about that here."

"You sure will. You'll learn how to market your business," said the teacher. "And a whole lot more. Like how to set up times for clients to come in. How to buy the things you need for the salon. How to manage other stylists. How to do the books. All that stuff. You'll even learn how to write a plan for your business."

A plan? Jackie had never had a plan. In her life, this had led to that and that had led to the next thing. She had never planned very far ahead.

So, as part of the Manager Course, Jackie wrote a business plan for her salon. She decided how much money she would try to make in the next two years. She decided what she would need to do to reach that point. She decided how much she would spend getting there.

Learning to run and market the business was a big part of the picture.

Jackie soaked it all up. Every time she got a new idea at school, she tried it out at home.

The first thing she did was change things around in the salon. She put up signs to tell clients everything she could do. She started selling shampoos and sprays and conditioners. She set up a stack of fancy bottles. Anyone walking in or out couldn't miss it. Of course, Rochelle knocked it over every other day. When that happened Jackie just built it back up again.

Jackie also started doing facials, manicures, and pedicures. People had asked about these things. Jackie just hadn't wanted to do them. Now she thought she had better do what clients asked for. There was money in them.

She also starting selling all-in-one deals. For one price, people could get their hair done, plus a facial and a manicure. The total cost was less than the cost of each one alone. Jackie was sort of surprised when people started buying the all-in-ones. She could fill a whole morning with just one person.

Since Jackie was doing manicures now, she started another special deal. Anyone who sent her three new clients got a free manicure. She did two free manicures that first month. That got her six new customers.

Then one day a woman called Jackie about buying an ad in the phone book. The ad could be small, so it wouldn't cost too much. The woman said it would surely bring her new business. The cost would be added to her phone bill each month.

Jackie decided to buy the ad. The woman helped her find just the right words for the small ad:

Jackie's Salon • 555-4601

Hair, Skin And Nail Care

That's Right For You

Jackie thought that said it all.

The Manager Course was over by the time the phone book came out. Jackie opened the book to the page with her ad on it. "There it is!" she cried. Everything looked just right. Now there was nothing to do but wait for new clients to call.

C H A P T E R   8

More Than Enough

Dance music played as Jackie wrapped thick cornrows around Taria's head. "Every time I do your hair it's a little more fancy than the last time!" Jackie laughed. "So tell me all about it. What fancy place are you going to this time?"

"My cousin's wedding," said Taria. "Robert's coming with me, of course."

"You two still not making your own plans, huh?" Jackie asked.

"Maybe next year," said Taria. "I want us to be really sure about each other before we get married."

"Really?" Jackie said. "Not like me the first time, huh?"

"Well, yeah, sort of," said Taria. "I mean, plenty of my friends tied up with the wrong guys. Some of them have babies and they're not doing too great. And you—well, you're doing fine now. But it wasn't easy, was it?"

"It's never easy," said Jackie. "But it's a whole lot harder when you have to raise a kid by yourself."

"And not everybody ends up as lucky as you," said Taria.

"Yeah," Jackie laughed. "You can say I'm lucky. But remember—I worked for what I have."

Taria started moving to the music.

"Hold still, honey," said Jackie. "I can't get this row straight if you're dancing!"

"The music makes me feel like I'm in a downtown salon," said Taria.

"I only have the dance music on for *you*," said Jackie. "Most of the time I play real soft music. If clients want a downtown salon, they have their pick. But if they want a nice, quiet salon, where no one but me sees them with goop in their hair, then Jackie's is the place to be."

Jackie finished Taria's hair. She handed her a mirror. "I love it!" cried Taria. "You're the best, Jackie!"

When the next woman came in, Jackie changed the music. After that a man came in. Then another woman came in just after the man left.

That's how all of Jackie's days were now—full. Her ad in the phone book was bringing in new business. So were the free manicures. Jackie had more clients than days to work on them. She was so busy, she had to book clients for two weeks ahead. She knew she could be making more money if her zoning permit let her work more days.

Then one day she was combing out a woman she first met at Hair Circus. "I miss going downtown to get my hair done," the woman said. "I wish you still worked at Hair Circus."

That put an idea in Jackie's head. Some of her clients would *rather* go downtown. And Jackie would rather work full-time than part-time.

The next day was one of the days she didn't work. She packed up Rochelle and caught a downtown bus. She went to see Alonzo at Hair Circus.

"Your baby! Your sweet baby!" Alonzo gushed when they walked in.

"She's not really a baby anymore!" said Jackie.

"Well, it's the first time I ever saw her. She's great!" said Alonzo. "So what can I do for you today?"

"I was thinking," said Jackie. "I have more work than I can fit into three days at home. Do you think I could work here two days a week?"

"You will not believe this!" said Alonzo. "Lila just asked me if she could cut back to three days a week. I said no. What would I do with an empty chair the other two days? But maybe you and Lila could work something out to fill up the week."

Lila had never been Jackie's favorite person. But Jackie took a minute to think about it. If she shared a job with Lila, they'd never be here at the same time.

Jackie walked over to talk with Lila. When Jackie left Hair Circus that day, she had a deal. Lila would work Wednesday, Friday, and Saturday. Jackie would work at Hair Circus every Tuesday and Thursday. She would work at her own salon on Wednesday, Friday, and Saturday. All the salons were closed on Mondays.

Now all Jackie needed was child care for Rochelle. That turned out to be easy, too. Jackie's mother wanted to take her. "It will be just like when Salina was little," her mother said. "I've been missing having a little one around."

And Jackie was glad to spend some time with Alonzo again, even if it was only two days a week.

CHAPTER 9

New Styles

"What's that noise?" Taria's mom asked. She looked up at the ceiling as Jackie held onto the roller in her hair.

"It's just Carl," said Jackie.

"Sounds like he's roller skating up there!" said Taria's mom.

"Our old wood floors are kind of loud," said Jackie.

"Well, just so he doesn't come down here," said Taria's mom. "I wouldn't want him to see me with a head full of rollers!"

Taria's mom didn't hear what Jackie was thinking. "It's *his* house, too," went through her mind. What Jackie said out loud was, "It's just one of those things when your business is at home."

Just then, Carl came down to get Rochelle. Taria's mom hid her face. "If you tell anyone you saw me looking like this, I'll never speak to you again!" she told Carl.

"Why don't I take a picture and show the world?" Carl laughed. He tried to be a good sport. But really, he often wished that people weren't coming in and out of his house all the time. Sometimes *he* felt like the one people were looking at.

"Hey, Jackie," said Taria's mom after Carl left. "Do you know how to do that new thing-a-ma-jig hairdo?"

"What's a thing-a-ma-jig?" Jackie laughed. "I've never heard of it."

"That's the name of the style," said Taria's mom. "I saw a picture in a magazine, and I want one for myself."

"I'm going to a class on new hairdos next week," said Jackie. "Maybe I'll learn how to do a thing-a-ma-jig."

The class was being held in the big city. Jackie had to take a train to get there. The trip was worth it. She not only learned to do a thing-a-ma-jig, but a few more new hairdos, too. She also learned about a new shampoo. She signed up to sell it in her salon.

Word got around fast that Jackie could do the thing-a-ma-jig. Taria's mom came running in to get hers. So did just about everyone else, it seemed. Jackie was so busy, she didn't know what to do. She had enough work to fill five days a week in her own salon and then some.

So she went back to the zoning board. She asked if she could work five days a week. The answer was still no.

"How about if I take on a second person?" she asked. "I could stay with three days a week if only I had help."

The answer to that one was no, too.

"Now what?" she said to Carl that night at dinner.

"Sounds like your home salon is holding you back," said Carl.

"It is, isn't it? But I don't want to rent a shop downtown. My idea was to be here, near the kids."

"Say you went out and found a shop to rent," Carl said. "Say you had all the space you need. Say you could work as many days as you wanted. Say you hired one or two more people. Are you ready for all that? Are you ready to be a salon manager?"

"I took the Manager Course."

"I know. But what I'm asking is this—are you ready to be the manager of a downtown salon?" Carl said.

"Everything's a step, isn't it?" said Jackie. "I guess running a downtown salon would be another step. My business plan was for two years. That two years is up."

"Are you ready for a new business plan?" Carl asked.

"I'm not sure," said Jackie. "I need to step back and take a long look at things."

CHAPTER 10

Sweet Dreams

The next morning, just for fun, Jackie looked in the paper under Stores for Rent. She saw three that looked interesting. She went by to see all three after work. Just for fun.

The first two were out of the question. The third one got Jackie's wheels turning again. As soon as she walked in, she could see herself working in that space. She could see two other stylists set up on the side. She could see a space for clients to sit while waiting their turn. She could see the walls covered with gold paper that wasn't even there. She could see a shiny black and white floor where now there was a dull green one. Everything about the place seemed right to her. Even the price.

"I'll think about it," she told the man who showed her around.

"Better think fast," said the man. "Shops on this block don't stay empty for long!"

"I'll think about it," Jackie said again.

She waited until the man drove away. Then she stepped into the shop next to the empty one.

"Don't let him get over on you," said the woman next door. "That shop's been empty for months."

"Oh, dear," Jackie said to herself. "If he's trying to get over on me now, what kind of landlord would he be?"

"He's OK," said the woman. "He's just

trying to get his price for the shop. Maybe you can work on him."

In just one day, Jackie had come close to renting the shop. She decided not to rush so fast. If she moved her salon downtown, she would have to make a lot of changes at home. She would have to leave Hair Circus—again. She wanted to think it all out before she jumped in.

She waited a week before calling the landlord. She decided that if he would take less rent, she would take the place. "Would you take 50 dollars less a month?" she asked him.

The landlord said yes. Jackie had a deal. She could hardly believe it.

Just then Taria ran into the salon. "I have big news! I thought I had ONE big thing to tell you, but I have TWO!"

"Let me guess," said Jackie.

She didn't have time to speak when Taria said, "Yes! Robert asked me to marry him! Next month he finishes trade school at last!"

"That's wonderful!" said Jackie.

Taria went on and on about her wedding plans. Then she said, "You'll do my hair for the wedding, won't you?"

"Of course, honey," said Jackie. "It will be my wedding gift to you!"

Taria hugged Jackie hard. Then she started to leave.

"Wait!" said Jackie. "What's the other thing you wanted to tell me?"

"Oh, I almost forgot! Remember when you told me to reach out and grab what I wanted? Well, I didn't ask Robert Tenby to marry me. But I *did* make up my mind about something else. I've decided to go to cosmetology school. I want to follow in your footsteps!"

Jackie grabbed Taria by both hands. "That's just great, honey! Now let me tell you *my* news! I'm moving my salon downtown! And you know what? Just as soon as you get your cosmetology license, I want you to work in my new place!"

Jackie and Taria were like two little

girls, jumping up and down. They hugged each other five or six more times. At last Taria said, "I gotta go. Put me down for the whole morning of my wedding day! I just know you are going to give me the hairstyle of the year!"

"I can't wait," said Jackie.

The next four months were busy like never before. Jackie got a bank loan to buy shampoo sinks, styling chairs and stations, a new floor, and gold wallpaper. Carl helped her fix up the new salon. Every night they worked on it. Jackie had a sign painted. *Jackie's,* it said in fancy gold letters. Below that the sign said *Salon of Style*.

She put an ad in the paper to tell everyone about the Grand Opening. She hung rows of gold ribbon across the shop.

"This place looks like prom night," said Taria's mom when she walked in. "And look at you, Jackie! You look like you're *at* the prom!"

Jackie was wearing the prom gown she

had kept all these years. It was purple with gold beads around the edges. Carl put his arm around her. "Let this *be* your prom night!" he told his wife. "You deserve it!"

Jackie couldn't remember ever feeling this happy. All that had happened came rushing through her head. Getting married and having a baby when she was still so young. Leaving school too soon. Getting her cosmetology license. Working at Hair Circus. Finding Carl. Starting her own salon at home. Having Rochelle. Building her business. Now this—a downtown salon of her own.

Yet Jackie knew these things had not just "happened" to her. She had *made* everything happen, through her own dreams and hard work.

"I'm dreaming," she said out loud. Her eyes were a little wet as she spoke.

"Are you all right?" Carl asked her.

"Oh, yes," said Jackie. "Nothing could be better than this. I just want to keep on dreaming, that's all. I can't ever let the dreaming slip away again."

Carl took Jackie's hand and held it tight. "Dream on!" he said to her softly.